THE REAL ACHIEVEMENT
OF VATICAN II

THE REAL ACHIEVEMENT OF VATICAN II

EDUARD SCHILLEBEECKX

TRANSLATED BY H. J. J. VAUGHAN

HERDER AND HERDER

1967
HERDER AND HERDER NEW YORK
232 Madison Avenue, New York 10016

Original edition: *Het tweede Vaticaans Concilie,*
Uitgeverij H. Nelissen, Bilthoven, 1966.

Nihil obstat: John Coventry, S.J., Censor
Imprimatur: ✠ Patrick Casey, Vicar General
Archdiocese of Westminster, November 7, 1966

Library of Congress Catalog Card Number: 67–25884
© 1967 by Sheed and Ward, Ltd.
Printed in the United States

CONTENTS

INTRODUCTION

Ever since the closing of the Second Vatican Council, there has been a growing keenness to ascertain the extent of its final decisions. Barely two months later there was already an amazingly wide demand for the council documents, not only from non-catholic Christians but also from agnostics, secularists and humanists, whose common desire was to make an exhaustive study of them. A journalist on a communist daily, in a talk with me on council matters, not only appeared well informed about the contents of the *Pastoral Constitution on the Church in the World of Today*, but was able to give an accurate assessment of the position with regard to the collegiality of the bishops, the new theological themes on the priestly office, etc. The fact is that, while some quarters kept up their reservations to the very end, on the assumption that certain matters would not be passed in the definitive, decisive session anyway, their interest in the final text took on considerable proportions once they were approved after all, and that without causing much harm. This is why I think it worthwhile enlarging on my earlier survey, in which I considered only the first and second stages of the council (1962–63).[1]

In this volume the third and fourth stages (1964–65) will be discussed from the same perspective and in the same spirit as the previous one. My concern is not with events and bits of information; these received ample mention in the world press. Religious thinking, the will of the church to take on a new aspect, the innermost spiritual tensions which showed up in the process—these are the things that hold my chief interest. As the council is now ended, the especial aim of this survey will be to cast an overall glance at the final result.

E. Schillebeeckx, OP

[1] This was published in America as *The Layman in the Church*, Staten Island, 1963.

1

THE THIRD SESSION

The third session of the Second Vatican Council can be divided into two overlapping, though not consecutive phases: one devoted to the amendment and final drafting, after repeated detailed and global voting, of schemas (a council term that could perhaps be rendered as "bill or draft for discussion in committee") which had already been discussed in previous sessions; and another in which entirely new schemas were first submitted to the council fathers for discussion. This is an important distinction for the generally "dry bones" of the so-called first phase had already been animated by the spirit of the council, whereas the others were no more than concepts which had not yet been geared by the bishops of the world into the very dynamics of the council. As a missionary bishop from Southern Rhodesia plainly put it in connection with the schema on *The Missionary Activity of the Church*, they were often presented to the council as nothing more than "dry bones".

The work of the third session proceeded at an exceptional tempo. The schemas awaiting attention were numerous and there was at first a widely held belief that this session would see the closing of the Second Vatican Council. This fast tempo did not, however, detract from the seriousness of the process of submission and assimilation of amendments to the schemas, nor did it lead to superficiality, for one month was enough to convince all and sundry that the third session could not possibly get through all the work. During the final weeks it became doubtful even whether the unofficially planned promulgation of five constitutions and decrees would take place at all; some of the commissions, indeed, had to reckon with anything between three and five thousand *modi* or amendments. Think of parliamentarians, after discussing a bill, having to take account of a dozen amendments from which to table a revised bill. Between the initial introduction and the final passing of the bill quite some time must inevitably be taken up by discussions, committee work, and study, and finally in weighing the various drafts. This is precisely what happened in the synod of the world's bishops. And when, moreover—as sometimes happened—a schema was completely rejected and the commission was faced with drafting an entirely new one, it became obvious that the council could not publish a dozen constitutions and decrees after every session, but at most one or two definitive documents.

The impatience of some of the faithful was understandable, therefore; these meetings, they said, had been going on for three full years and the mountain had brought forth a mouse. But when one was taking part in the council's activities, one could only applaud this procedure. The council had everything to gain from a ripening process; we ought to think of a great French wine cellar from which there emerges at length a matured wine in which one can taste the vintage year. It is, after all, unthinkable that, for instance, what the bishops said in the council hall during the third session, could have been expressed in the second. Furthermore, an incident like the following would have been inconceivable a year ago: the pope, animated with the best intentions but apparently badly informed, called at the council hall on 6 November and gave it as his opinion that the schema on the missions was a sound one requiring only slight touching-up and shading here and there; but in spite of this, the following day the council fathers, to loud and repeated applause from the entire assembly, with salvos of truth revealing hammer blows, torpedoed this project as being unworthy of the council. The vast majority of the bishops were truly sensitive to the needs of mankind and of the church. They were not intent on giving the people stones and scorpions instead of the bread they were clamouring for. This is the light in which I regard the Second Vatican Council. The few catholics, both laymen and priests, who declared themselves loath even to read the reports on the council, since they expected no good to come of it, were only showing their ignorance and sad lack of perception, understandable at times but never justifiable from a Christian viewpoint.

Naturally, a council offers a chance for the office of the church to express its collective awareness (supported, for that matter, by the collective awareness of all the faithful and by the common self-awareness characteristic of our day and age), which, like any other collective awareness, has developed from ever-changing majority and minority views. The minority, too, has its rights. What it comes down to is this: the definitive documents of the council never can and never will be an accurate reflection of the vision of the "open wing" which was the majority. To some extent the council documents unavoidably lag behind these visions and apostolic yearnings of the bishops. This is yet another point to be borne in mind by the faithful who still expect great things as the final result of the council. The church, as God's living people, is more than a council, after all.

I am convinced, nevertheless, that the consequences of the definitive council decisions which have already been reached will prove incalculable.

Though decades may pass before there is clear evidence of it, I am sure that the life of the church will change considerably as a result (for instance) of the collegiality of the bishops or of the chapter devoted to God's people in the *Constitution on the Church,* or of the decree on the catholic contribution to the ecumenical movement.

In this survey of the third session I cannot possibly touch upon all the themes that were discussed, not even those of the *Dogmatic Constitution on the Church* and the two decrees promulgated during that session.

I would far sooner try to explain what is going on in the church due to the council. What I have in mind is not the minor and major difficulties and the backstage wire-pulling; in the heat of the struggle for one's personal views which others do not share, self-control is not a fact but rather a task. These difficulties have to some extent become common knowledge through the press, but in the whole of the actual council event they were no more than marginal occurrences. What I mean is that we must look for the significance in salvation history of what is being accomplished in the church and has penetrated through the council into wide layers of the hierarchy of the church. For this is clear: the will to steer a new course, though guided by the compass of the evangelical, apostolic church and her scriptures, witness of the unique fact of the redemption wrought by God in Christ, is something that has struck believers and atheists alike. What is the meaning of this change of course? Especially, what is its saving-historical significance on the *kairos,* i.e. the moment in the present world situation prepared by God's redeeming love?

Christianity rediscovered as an event

The press has shown how certain non-Christian circles think of this council. They regard it not as a real change of course but rather as a diplomatic change of front, a tactical move, a new and clever manœuvre to regain the sympathy of a world which is no longer Christian as in the Middle Ages or during the Ancien Régime but an enfranchised, secularised and even dechristianised world. The former strongholds of the church have obviously crumbled away. This is how those circles interpret the situation: in the past, when the church occupied temporal key positions, she sang the triumph of the one true church who alone had the right to expand as a church in the world; but now that she finds herself in a minority position—only eighteen per cent of the world population being catholic—she is intent, from tactical political considerations, on striking up a different tune, a song to captivate the heart of non-catholics. But, they say, this is only a new trick to play up to those

6

who have become estranged from the church, for behind this smoke-screen the church continues straight on her old course. The wrapping has been changed and modernised but the contents are still stones and scorpions, not lifegiving bread.

Certainly, when we read some of the statements in the schemas awaiting approval, we had to admit that the church herself is sometimes responsible for creating this misunderstanding; and there was a suggestion of a certain opportunism. But it is remarkable that the vast majority of the bishops reacted strongly against it. What was particularly noticeable in St Peter's was a tendency to give preference to the historical truth without, however, straining the theoretical or speculative truth. A few instances will clarify this.

The original schema on the eastern churches contained the sentence: "The Catholic Church has always held the Eastern Churches in high regard." As a speculative truth this is correct, i.e. the existence of the universal church implies this esteem; but, historically speaking, it is simply untrue, for these churches have had much to endure from changing curial diplomacy. Similarly, Schema 13 (the former Schema 17 on *The Church in the World of Today*) stated that the church has always appreciated, encouraged and promoted culture, science and progress. This is obviously a true implication of the correct relation between the church and the world; but, from a historical

7

view-point, the church has, in fact, also done the reverse—she has also slowed down science and progress. Now, it was characteristic of the council that the bishops gave evidence of greater sensitivity to the historical dimension of the church, the faith and the Christian life. It is no coincidence, therefore, that it was also the first council to advance—in the constitution on revelation—the development of tradition as an essential aspect of the entire religious life of the church.[1] Earlier councils have obliquely affirmed this dogmatic development, but the direct intention was to state that the contents of faith in all this development remain unchangeable. Now, however, the emphasis is rather that the faith remains identical with itself, dynamically, in its growth.

What could, in the constitution on revelation, still look like a mere affirmation of speculative truth is in practice carried through in all the episcopal interventions. Thus, many bishops have asked that on the question of "church and world" the council should affirm not only the speculative but also the historical truth—for instance, that there was a time when the church held the world under her tutelage and that, while she then con-

[1] The *Dogmatic Constitution on Divine Revelation*, finally promulgated on 18 November 1965 (see p. 92 below), is one of the most important fruits of the council. It was the original preconciliar schema on revelation which, on its dramatic rejection at the first session in 1962, created the division between council majority and minority. See further pp. 39–41 below.

8

tributed much to mankind's earthly welfare, she often also hindered the rightful emancipation of the world and the progress of culture and was not unprejudiced towards the earnest quest for truth in every field. Obviously the history of the church should not be judged by the modern standards of a changed world situation; nevertheless, many council Fathers insisted that the church also affirm this historical truth and, therefore, express her sorrow over past errors. For the rest, from a pastoral viewpoint, the church would increase her moral and spiritual authority if she were to simply acknowledge that she is invariably cloaked in the garb of historical truth and does not always want to appear in the festive dress of speculative truth which many, believers included, regard as a half lie.

Quite often the clashes between the minority and majority views at the council could virtually —and possibly even essentially—be reduced to this tension between the recognition of the historical and that of the speculative truth or, let us say, to the definition of the essence of the church. There were those who couldn't realise that the essence of the church can never show up other than in historical form. This incapacity is, remarkably, expressed in two ways: either the historical truth is suppressed, or the essence of the church is identified with this historical truth. Especially in the discussions on episcopal collegiality, and even after its acceptance in principle, there remained a certain blindness to the distinction between historical and speculative truth. The minority view identified the dogmatic primacy of the pope, embedded in episcopal collegiality, with its concrete, in part purely historically conditioned, form; one which, in some respects, is really beginning to look like what the reformation termed "papalism". Here historical truth is treated as speculative. I am convinced that the basic reason for the continuing opposition of an ever decreasing but tough minority lies in its blindness to historical truth, in contrast with the modern world, which adopts the historicity of all that is human as its main dogma; one which, come to that, occasionally swings over to dogmatism even here.

This same phenomenon occurred in the controversial discussions on the schema on the catholic principles of ecumenism. The champions of purely speculative truth stubbornly insisted on recognising only the Catholic Church as the one true, holy and apostolic church and on denying all ecclesial significance to the non-catholic Christian denominations. However, given this supreme speculative truth, the council document on ecumenism has also soberly recognised the historical truth that the non-catholic Christian religions undoubtedly contain evangelical basic elements of the one true church of Christ, while, on the other hand, though historically speaking truly evangelical and ecclesial-theological elements were never of course denied by the Catholic Church, in the ordinary life of the church they have got and get little chance. To be consistent, the protagonists of purely speculative truth, which they consider detached from history, as it were, can only speak of the return of all other Christian churches to the one true church of Roman Catholicism, whereas those who claim that truth is historical (the position of the *Decree on Ecumenism*) apply this idea of a "return" just as much to the actual, historical Catholic Church itself—not as if the true, universal church of Christ did not exist at all and will only come about as the result of a supra-confessional, "new church" of Christ, towering above all existing Christian churches; but that through another, more evangelical form of the Catholic Church, the other Christian churches will regard themselves and act as this Catholic Church. There will be, then, a real growing together until at length they can recognise themselves in each other—and this without in any way violating either speculative or historical truth.

In the same vein instances of this tension could be quoted in connection with every schema. The emotion which was unmistakable in many episcopal interventions finds its source in the closeness to life of bishops with an eye for man as a concrete being and for what is actually happening in the world, who ask themselves how the Church, precisely because of her messianic mission, should be involved in these events. I would say that the characteristic of this council was not abstract truth, or doctrinal definitions, but actuality. Not that the truth had become secondary or "something to suppress"—that would be disloyal—but that the bishops' chief preoccupation was the way Christian truth is to be accomplished: How is it to become an event in the concrete world of man today? It was precisely because of this preoccupation that the schema on the priestly ministry was outvoted and that the council fathers asked for an entirely new one. To be sure, this rejected schema had said many true things about the priesthood but it had done so merely on the level of speculative truth. Hardly anything was said about the pastoral questions which lie heavily on many priests and create unrest and uncertainty in the care of souls; as if an abstract description of a priest, priestly holiness and priestly apostolate dealt exhaustively with the problem. This applied even more clearly to the schema on the missionary activity of the church; in addition, it lacked vitality and life-blood and was accordingly outvoted by the council fathers in spite of delicate circumstances.

This should not lead to the conclusion that the council favoured a sort of activism. It was well aware that Christianity is not merely an ideological or doctrinal system, but must also be an event in which real salvation history is enacted? Sounds like these which rang through certain interventions found a pure echo in the *Constitution on Divine Revelation*. Whereas the old schema on the "two sources" of revelation, which was withdrawn as long ago as the first session, called revelation, in the final analysis, a divine communication of a number of truths which surpass man's understanding—suggesting a rather conceptualistic view—the new constitution sees revelation as something more personal and as part of a history of salvation—as a saving-historical event which is inwardly clarified by God's prophetic word, an event which makes history and accordingly has a beginning, a development and a fulfilment in the historical appearance of the man Jesus, the Son of God, the consummation of the faith. Moreover, the tradition of the faith in church history was also geared into the same dynamics. What was formerly meant by it was almost exclusively the passing on by word of mouth of the church's doctrine; in this constitution it becomes a living tradition, not only of a doctrine but also of the saving realities themselves. Tradition is the very life of the entire church under the inspiration of the Holy Ghost—a view which prompted the eastern bishop Mgr Edelby to say that just as holy scripture is the consecration of salvation history, so tradition is its epiclesis. Thus church

13

tradition does not transmit first and foremost, for instance, a doctrine on the eucharist but the living reality of the eucharistic celebration itself, the living and saving reality, whose doctrine is but an elucidation of its inner significance. Because the apostolic tradition of the church means loyalty to revelation through the ages, to that revelation which was accomplished in Christ, according to the testimony of the apostles deposited in the scriptures, the council decree states: "The preaching of the church and the Christian religion itself should always look up to Scripture as the model and the authority by which they are led and (critically) judged" (Chap. 6 No. 21). This means that the Catholic Church has in principle definitively abandoned the anti-protestant bias of her post-Tridentine theology.[1] I could go on like this and point out this modern and at the same time Christian feeling for the historical, mutable dimension of human existence and of the Christian faith in every new accent of all the various conciliar constitutions, declarations and decrees.

Christianity is again regarded and experienced

---

[1] Unfortunately the text lost much of its force, at least in its formulation, owing to the adoption of an amendment by the Theological Commission: "The preaching of the church and the Christian religion itself must always be sustained by scripture". Note the addition from the fourth session, after the original publication of this article: the definitive text reads: "are sustained and guided by scripture".

as a dynamic event, not merely as the sum total of a number of doctrinal points. The so-called pastoral character of this council is nothing but a new dogmatic sensitivity. It would be a fundamental misconception, therefore, to consider this church assembly less doctrinal than the earlier ones, just because of its pastoral tendency. Some of those who hold minority views will be making a sad mistake if they accept the final decisions of this council "because it is, after all, only pastoral", as if everything were to remain unchanged as far as doctrinal presentation is concerned. I have a feeling that the theologians will undoubtedly be faced with such a post-conciliar interpretation of some of the council decisions.

Definitive formulation of the concept of collegiality

Although mention has already been made of collegiality,[1] this question must be looked into again in the light of the definitive text. In actual fact, the council only approved an ontological collegiality, a static and mysterious reality which lies dormant in the lap of the church. Collegiality, insofar as the council has accepted it, is undoubtedly a theological reality, consisting, however, in a real potential that waits, perhaps with

[1] See above, esp. pp. 9–10.

impatience and longing, to see whether the pope is going to invoke it. The *nota praevia* or explanatory note has done no more, in fact, than formulate a possibility which was present in the third chapter of the *Constitution on the Church*, though not brought out in the text itself. Anyone making a close study of the official *relatio* (or explanatory memorandum) on the third chapter, drafted by Mgr Parente, and of the defence by the Theological Commission of the unaccepted *modi*, or amendments (which had, as a matter of fact, already been drafted before there was any mention of an "explanatory supplementary note"), must come to the conclusion that there is no great difference between them and the possibility presented in the constitution itself. The latter did not go quite so far as the so-called new theology of episcopal collegiality, but did not expressly say so. In the constitution itself, indeed, we come across two titles in connection with the pope: he is "the chief pastor of the whole church" and he is "head of the college". But nowhere do we find either affirmation or denial that these two titles are really distinct. Moreover, it appears from a reply of the Theological Commission to a rejected amendment that the commission left undecided the question whether the prerogative of "chief pastor" formally rests on that of "head of the college". The council itself has not, therefore, pronounced on this point. This means that, disregarding even the "explanatory note", the constitution has approved the collegiality of the bishops (between themselves and in hierarchic communion with the pope), but neither affirms nor denies that of the pope himself as the chief pastor of the church. The door was, therefore, left ajar; no more than that. In the explanatory note, by contrast, a clear distinction is made between those two titles. The conclusion is obvious: the voting on 16 November, seen in the light of the explanatory note, undoubtedly approved the bishops' collegiality but not the pope's.

I feel, however, that this does not exhaust the historical and scientific interpretation of the doctrine of collegiality. For, although the voting was officially and juridically coupled with the "explanatory note", remarkable things have taken place in the minds of the voters. Questioned individually on the significance of their vote, many council fathers replied that they had voted for chapter III as such, without the slightest intentional reference to the explanatory note. This will no doubt puzzle future historians of the council. It was not the council fathers' intention to exclude all further evolution.

The conclusion may be justified that in the matter of collegiality the council is but a link in a still continuing dogmatic development. A great step forward has been made, compared with the First Vatican Council, for the bishops' collegiality

17

was explicitly defined as an ecclesial, onto-logical reality which is already present in the church, at least as an active possibility, on the basis of the sacramental mystery. What was not defined is the collegiality of the pope as chief pastor of the whole church and this lies at the very heart of the modern theology of collegiality and was, no doubt, alive also in the thoughts of many council fathers. For the rest, the life of the church goes on developing even after the end of a council.

If I were asked now about papal collegiality in post-conciliar practice, my reply, paradoxical though it may sound, would be that the voting will promote rather than hinder it. If, in spite of every-thing, the affirmation of papal collegiality had been won from a minority (which does, in fact, exist), the pope would have been placed in a position, after the council, where he was com-pelled to give constant proof to the minority that the papal primacy has in no way suffered from the new definition. Now, on the contrary, his position is that he must constantly prove that his papal authority does not harm the bishops' col-legiality. More than ever, the pope's senate stands a good chance of coming into being. When we look at the story of the "explanatory note" from an ecclesio-sociological point of view, what has happened (as an explanation after the fact, of course) could well turn out to be providential through human interventions. In the church of Christ theology is not everything, thank God. We often see that it is not theory that engenders practice, but that, on the contrary, it is the practice of the church which eventually clarifies the doctrine and causes it to be unanimously accepted. The practice of papal collegiality, stimulated by the social law which is unavoidably set in motion by the restraining "explanatory note", could prove a greater blessing than a conciliar definition of the pope's collegiality (as head of the church) which might give rise to all kinds of psychological and sociological protective reactions because of the reality of the minority position.

Belief in God, belief in man

Besides the council's underlying tendency to stress historical truth while still upholding speculative truth there is yet another basic concern that requires elucidation: the attempt to integrate belief in man with belief in God. Particularly since the seventeenth century and the origin of "natural theology" in a rather rationalist form, there has been a breach between theology and anthropology, between God and the world, between the church and mankind. And it stands to reason that, owing to the dialectics of history, a period of religion without the world and without humanity was soon followed by a period in which the world and humanity were without a God.

Schema 13, which has gained notoriety in the meantime, had shown a certain sensitivity to this problem but, on that score anyway, it turned out rather poor. However, it shared the common lot of schemas born and developed in a limited commission: only after a schema had gone through the mill of the general assemblies in St Peter's, i.e. when the bishops of the world had expressed their views on the problem submitted, was it geared into the dynamism of the council. Only then did it become a good schema. It is no doubt true that not a single bishop brought up in the council chamber the problem of our time, as expressed, for instance, by Bishop Robinson of Woolwich and materially shared by many Christians besides him. Nevertheless, the problem was felt to be reflected in some of the interventions, betraying the council fathers' keenness to bridge the rift between the church and the world. Hence the council's great interest in the problems of world hunger, racial discrimination and the development areas, and in a social-economic and political order in which it is possible to lead a fully human, Christian life. Some of the bishops have accused the theologians—at times prophetically —of continuing to use technical language and terms that are strange to the world and beyond the people's comprehension.

This is true too of the outward appearance of the church. The form occasionally used in addressing the council fathers by the latinist Mgr Felici, the council's general secretary, "patres ornatissimi" (literally: "ornate, embellished council fathers", but in classical Latin equivalent to "highly honoured" council fathers, in itself neither more nor less Byzantine than, for instance, "Your Excellency"), drew from Archbishop Henrique Golland of Botucatu (Brazil), the following reaction in the council hall: "That is what the people also call us, though in a different sense, when they see us bishops walking through the streets polished and arrayed from head to toe" (109th General Assembly, 26 October, 1964). And the bishop implored the pope to allow them to come to the hall each morning in a plain black cassock. True, such customs amount almost to folk lore; but the reaction betrays a sensitivity on the part of the fathers to reality and to the way the people actually look at the church, as well as a desire to avoid anything that makes it more difficult for them to discover the real saving significance of the church. They want to purge the church of anything that gives her the appearance of a kind of ideological superstructure on concrete human life, for anything resembling a "superstructure" is unsuitable for clarifying Christianity's real transcendence; on the contrary, it unavoidably draws a wrong picture of the transcendence of the church which, though endowed with its own special and autonomous vital principles based on God's saving plan and its positive institution by Christ, lives in the people, with the people and with the world. A little work by an unknown third-century father of the church, the "Letter to Diognetes," gives a very good description of the present views of many council fathers: "Christians are indistinguishable from other men, either by their place of residence, by their speech or by their clothes. They do not live in separate towns, their dialect is not out of key, there is nothing special about their way of life . . . They settle in the Greek and the non-Greek (barbarian) towns as the fancy takes them; they adapt themselves to the local customs as regards clothing, food and way of life. And yet they bear witness to the special, really paradoxical rules of life of their own 'politeia' (spiritual fatherland) . . . They fulfil all their civic duties . . . marry and have children . . . Live in the flesh but not according to the flesh . . . They obey the established laws but their mode of life puts these laws in the shade . . . In one word: Christians are in the world what the soul is in the body".[1] It is easy to render this in modern idiom.

In conclusion, a concrete statement of the tendencies manifested in the bishops' interventions in connection with Schema 13 on church and world will reveal the main lines of the final draft. Just as there is a dogmatic development in the

[1] "A Diognète," trans. H. J. Marrou, *Sources Chrétiennes*, no. 33, Paris 1951, 63 and 65.

tradition of the faith, there is an evolution in the attitude of the church to the world in the course of her history. Indeed, the church cannot foresee all the implications of the redemption. She too learns from the developments in profane history with its ever-changing historical situations. Thus she herself makes salvation history. History itself is not, indeed, merely the outward framework, the disturbances of the times that flow past the church without touching her. Her very being is involved in these historical events which thus become historical events just as much of the church as of the world outside. The dialogue of the faith with mankind enables the former— modelled by Christ's unique appearance in this world, to which the apostolic church testifies in her scriptures—to take its place in history in a gradual development process which, after much hesitation and searching, releases the inner riches of the faith with increased clarity. Thus it strikes us, for instance, in church history how in periods of estrangement between the church and the world, the former appeals especially to secular media and temporal positions of strength for the fulfil-ment of her spiritual mission in the world. By contrast, when such estrangement is either non-existent or about to be removed, the church abandons these temporal positions of strength and prefers to appear as the truly evangelical church whose position in the world is without temporal support and, from a secular viewpoint, one of disarmed helplessness. Nevertheless, it is only then that she appears as a mighty, irresistible sign. In the helplessness of the cross also lay the power of Jesus, the servant of God and men, exalted now by the Father himself as the lord of the world.

The renewed self-awareness of the church and the new, human and Christian appraisal of the world demand that the church redefine its position towards the secularised world. To this new appraisal Schema 13 must solemnly bear witness. And the starting-point for it is obvious. What, in fact, do we see going on in the world? Man is making mighty efforts to turn the world situation into a truly human situation—actions which ought to compel the church's joyful admiration. The church, moreover, observes how great worldly undertakings succeed one day and fail the next; and how, despite these ups and downs, mankind sets to work again and again on the exacting task of the world's human development. A veiled hope appears to inspire and drive this world, a hope that endures despite signs of despair and of the senselessness of world history. In Schema 13 the church must, "always . . . be prepared to make a defence to any one who calls (it) to account for the hope that is in (it)" (1 Pt 3:15), bring this hidden hope into the light of day and invite the world to her positive hope: "If you knew the gift of God" (Jn 4:10), from which the world unconsciously draws life. If the world only knew God's gift!

Schema 13 must, therefore, without falling into false human optimism, become the Magna Charta of Christian hope which also draws every human aspiration into her purifying and uplifting dynamism. The church indeed loves the world, not only insofar as it is susceptible to grace, but also for itself. Its love for the world is a true love; it is creative and benevolent. And this is why the church wants the world to have the great human values which it so badly needs: freedom of conscience, the personal dignity of marriage and family, the cultural values, a social-economic and political organisation in which it is possible to lead a truly human, Christian life and, finally, a world community living in order and peace. No doubt, the relationship between the world's human development and the new heaven and earth surpasses all human and even religious thinking: "no eye has seen, nor ear heard, nor the heart of man conceived, what God has prepared for those who love him" (1 Cor. 2:9). This is why the final significance of the world's human development fades into the mystery which is accessible only to the faith that raises the hope expressed in Rev 21:3–4:

Behold the dwelling of God is with men. He will dwell with them, and they shall be his people, and God himself will be with them; he will wipe away every tear from their eyes, and death shall be no more, neither shall there be mourning nor crying nor pain any more, for the former things have passed away.

This is what Schema 13 must proclaim and celebrate and in that perspective of the eschatological final fulfilment the faithful who already have the pledge and the guarantee of the Holy Ghost and, therefore, of the eschatological gift, must labour on the world's constant restoration despite the reality of sin which never ceases to undermine redemption's work. But this redemption will make the world into an abode worthy of man and of God's people.

2

THE GAINS
FROM VATICAN II

Before turning our attention to the basic outlook
of the council as a whole, it may be useful to sum-
marise its really new achievements in the fields of
faith and theology; to consider, in other words,
how much has been officially accepted of what
may well have been alive among the faithful—
theologians and others—long before the council
but could, at that time at least, neither appeal to
the church's teaching authority nor look to the
hierarchy for support. Without entering into a
detailed analysis, brief mention will be made only
of what is "new" in most of the constitutions, decrees and declarations. If these details are singled
out, it is not to suggest that only innovations are
important, but so that long-standing Christian
possessions may also live anew in us.

Constitution on the Sacred Liturgy

1. The fundamental gain of this constitution is
that it broke the clergy's monopoly of the liturgy.
Whereas it was formerly the priest's affair, with

the faithful no more than his clientèle, the council regards not only the priest but the entire Christian community, God's people, as the subject of the liturgical celebration, in which each in his proper place is given his own particular, hierarchically ordered function—a theological view with all kinds of practical repercussions.

2. Partly in the light of this basic vision, three renewals become intelligible: the vernacular in the liturgy, the restoration of communion under two kinds, and concelebration. These are logical consequences of the renewed communal conception of the liturgy as the celebration of the entire Christian community in accordance with the *taxis* or hierarchical ordering of all the participants.

3. Moreover, the "theology of the word" was restored to its "quasi sacramental" importance. The revival of the liturgy of the word in general and particularly in the eucharist is its logical consequence.

4. In connection with the eucharist, the council relinquished the old sacrificial concept common to various religions and reached out direct to the biblical and ecclesial sacrificial concept, with the paschal mystery as its centre.

5. Finally, the rigid post-Tridentine uniformity was abandoned in favour of the principle of pluralism, especially for groups of different cultures.

1. In contrast with the old commentaries on the church, whose starting-point was an analysis of "the nature of the church", the guiding principle now is: the mystery of the church as shown by the varied imagery of the bible. Whereas theology previously gave its preference to "notions" or abstract concepts, the "image" as a means of elucidating that mystery has come into its own again.

2. The council has restored one of the basic convictions shared by all Christian churches: that Christ is the centre of the church. The church is not regarded as a static quantity, but projected on the screen of salvation history against the background of the *consilia Dei*, the economy of salvation of the Father through the Son in the Spirit. No other council has given the concept of "historia salutis", redemptive history, such obvious predominance in all its documents.

3. The idea of "God's kingdom" has re-entered into catholic theology. The church is not simply identified with it. This explains the dialectics of whether salvation has "already" or "not yet" been achieved in the church, and therefore her eschatological tension. Compared with the church's "official" doctrine before the council, all this is new. Furthermore, a distinction was drawn—and with what subtle finesse!—between the mystery

of "the church of Christ" and the actual aspect of the Roman Catholic Church; a distinction which was partly made in recognition of the ecclesial character of non-catholic Christian communities.

4. The church is in the first place "God's people", whereas in the past "church" was almost invariably identified with the ecclesiastical hierarchy. I feel that this new point will most forcibly affect the shaping of the church's future. This people is a "messianic people" with a charismatic, prophetic and priestly character, bearing witness to the lordly or royal redemptive omnipotence of Christ, the lord, the Kyrios.

5. Belonging to the church is no longer given a univocal significance but an analogous one, so that, in a whole range of different gradations, everyone, including even a well-disposed agnostic, has some connection with this church and is not a complete outsider. Thus the council surpassed the narrower view of the encyclical letter *Mystici Corporis*.

6. Within this people of God there are various clerical and lay functions; but there is also the special ecclesiastical ministry of the official priesthood: the pope and the bishops, the priests (presbyters) and the deacons. This ecclesiastical ministry, though differing in its essence from the priesthood of all the faithful, is a ministerial function precisely towards this universal priest-

hood, which is essentially related to it. There is no question, therefore, of a radical contrast between the two; they bring about a cooperative unity. The revival of the idea that the ecclesiastical ministry, though really governing the church, is at its service (*diakonia*) invokes the censure of holy scripture on all clerical pretensions. Of all these innovations, the restoration of the "substantive diaconate" and even of married deacons is the most striking. But particularly new and hopeful is the fact that the council has given its approval to episcopal collegiality; under the guiding principle of papal primacy the bishops as a group are the highest leadership of the church. The collegial government of the church has thus been approved in principle by the council.

7. A new official achievement undoubtedly is the view that all hierarchical mission is based on consecration; juridical competence and teaching authority too are based on consecration itself, and not merely on the so-called power of orders. Thus the ancient *sacerdotium* concept has been completely restored and is no longer merely identified with the ceremonial priesthood.

8. By restoring to every bishop the ancient title of "vicar of Christ" (*vicarius Christi*), which had been reserved for the pope since about the eighth century, the council lays the foundation for a "theology of the local church", in which the

universal church is represented; though any tendency towards diocesan "insularity" is denounced by the collegiality idea: every religious community is open to the whole body.

9. Because of the collegiality principle, including that of the church's teaching authority, the First Vatican Council's rather juridically expressed formulation that papal definitions are infallible *ex sese* (of themselves) will now (Second Vatican Council) take on a different function in the life of the church.

10. With regard to Mariology, the council, by incorporating the Marian mystery in the mystery of the church (and, accordingly, in this dogmatic constitution), may well put a brake on excessive theological tendencies, although its aim is not to detract from dogmatically founded true Marian devotion.

11. New also, to a certain extent, is the express affirmation that all are called to holiness, which is not a monopoly of the religious.

12. Finally, although the term is not used, the church is *sacramentum mundi*, the sacrament of the world, "sign and instrument of unity among men". Thus church and world are brought into contact and the *Pastoral Constitution on Church and World* is ushered in—a remarkable expression which appears in the very first paragraph of this dogmatic constitution.

1. Among the most important new affirmations is the statement that there is no specifically catholic ecumenical movement alongside the great ecumenical movement which was instituted in the World Council of Churches. The Catholic Church, taking her stand on her catholic faith, participates in the one great movement whose aim is the establishment of the one church of the *Oikoumenē*, in complete loyalty to the biblical mystery of "the church of Christ".

2. Other non-catholic Christian communities are also called churches or ecclesial communities, and no longer termed "sects" or heretical communities. The Catholic Church recognises that they have much in common with her.

3. The criterion of comparison between the various churches is not the Roman Catholic Church as such, but the apostolic fullness, the fullness of the messianic promise. In other words, the decree is a successful synthesis of true ecumenism and the conviction of the catholic faith that it really possesses this apostolic fullness, though veiled and always open for further purification.

4. The idea of a dialogue "on an equal footing" cannot go unmentioned as a new attitude on the part of catholics.

5. In this connection an important pronouncement is made, which, as a conciliar statement,

is certainly new: there is hierarchy in the truths of faith. This is an implicit reaction, for instance, against exaggerated Marian preaching as well as against any preaching which, in contrast with the protestant confession of Christ, leaves the central religious truths in the shade and gives preference to peripheral ones.

6. The affirmation that both doctrinal and liturgical expressions are not tied down to the conceptual formulae of the Latin West is, from the official church's viewpoint, a new and important pronouncement.

7. The praying together of Christians from different churches and an already far-reaching participation in each other's religious celebrations should not be omitted from this enumeration.

Finally, the very existence of this decree as a council document is in itself something new in the tradition of the Catholic Church.

Decree on the Eastern Catholic Churches

1. Although neither eastern nor western Christians are very happy about this council document, one point at least can be brought to the fore: the concept of the patriarchate which has, for all practical purposes, been lost in the western church, may in the future, precisely by its function in the church, contribute more than episcopal collegiality to a closer definition of what is the

bishop of Rome's due as pope, what as patriarch of the West. The historical identification of these two functions has brought confusion in the relation between the papacy and the eastern churches.

2. For the rest, this document is important as a basis for analogy arguments in approaches to other Christian churches, for instance, on the subject of the refusal of rebaptism and participation in each other's religious worship.

Decree on the Pastoral Office of Bishops in the Church

This decree is especially important for ecclesiastical structures. These are its new points:

1. In the extension of the bishops' collegial direction of the church, though not coincidental with it, lies the "synod of bishops", officially desired by the council and in the meantime instituted by the pope, whose purpose it is to hold regular meetings between councils to discuss with the pope important problems of the church and of local churches, either on a consultative or on a decisive basis, to be determined by the pope.

2. In line with it, too, is the decision to involve residential bishops in the official curial bodies, as is also the internationalisation of the latter.

3. Entirely new is the view of the juridical competence of the local bishop. Whereas in the

past there was a list of things bishops were permitted to do (in other words, the point of departure was the derivation of their power from the pope), the most we can look for now is a list of matters in which the pope, in the interest of the whole church, continues to curtail the bishops' official competence in this or that detail; the starting-point now is the idea that the bishop, on the ground of his consecration, fundamentally possesses every official competence necessary to act as a real leader of his community.

4. The bishops' national, provincial and supranational conferences have been officially confirmed as a structural principle in the new church order. In addition, with a view to effective pastoral planning and coordination, the wish is explicit that the superiors of religious orders should on occasion send their delegates to attend these bishops' conferences.

5. Another new structural principle is the institution of the local bishops' pastoral advisory council, composed of both clerics and laymen. According to this decree, the clerical members are selected by the bishop himself, though according to the decree on the ministry and life of priests it is they who choose their representatives on the bishop's advisory council. From the concept that the church is a community, episcopal collegiality is carried through in a downward line—although

collegiality here does not have the same theological meaning, as it does not refer to office directly.

6. Finally, there is novelty also in the fact that this council document demands a certain revision of the status of papal nuncios; what is required is, at least, the internationalisation of their corps, as well as a better and closer definition of their task.

Decree on Training for the Priesthood

1. New, to some extent, in this not entirely successful document is the fact that at least a certain pluralism has been allowed in the formation of the candidates for the priesthood.

2. An important innovation here is the *ratio studiorum* or the arrangement of the curriculum. Henceforth the studies are to start off with a global initiation in salvation history, a kind of overall saving-historical picture of the redemptive mystery in which we are living. This is followed by philosophy, which must, in its contents at least, be synchronised with theology. Philosophy must be centred on man, his world and God. Moreover, the progress of present-day philosophy should be taken into account and attention drawn to both the difference and the connection between man's philosophical self-appraisal and his religious outlook. Theology itself must have a biblical and patristic foundation,

and from that foundation, and that alone, go on to develop new directions open to the needs of the modern world. New also is the fact that this arrangement of the curriculum is not regarded as a definitive rule but incorporates the principle of continual *aggiornamento* in the rule itself.

Declaration on Christian Education

This declaration cannot be said to contain anything new in the sense I attach to this term.

Declaration on the Relation of the Church to Non-Christian Religions

Both in tenor and in tendency, this entire declaration is something of a real innovation in the official church. I shall revert to it in my synthetic survey of the Second Vatican Council; it will be sufficient, therefore, to mention a few salient points here.

1. The church acknowledges the "religious experience" which is the basis of the world's non-Christian religions. She regards mankind's religious problem as being intimately interwoven with the problem of man's existence. Thus the declaration constitutes an incipient new attitude to the adherents of those religions and, more especially, a first step in a sincere but prudent dialogue with them.

2. Although the declaration gives no "theology of Israel", it does, nevertheless, give a fundamen-

tal explanation of the intimate links between Israel and the church; one more reason for the church's solemn dissociation from all forms of anti-semitism which was partly fostered by the unqualified representation of "the Jews" as deicides. In very measured terms "the Jews" of those days are now declared innocent, although the contention remains that, others apart, some Jews had a share in Jesus' death.

Decree on Social Mass Media

Although it is an entirely new departure for a council to occupy itself with factors like these this decree can hardly be said to teach us anything exciting. It is not sufficiently well thought out technically, and too moralising, for that. As the council fathers' attention was focussed on more pressing religious problems at the time, they gave this immature decree their grudging approval.

Dogmatic Constitution on Divine Revelation

This dogmatic constitution is in many ways the council's crown jewels. Its theme was the root cause of the division which sprang up during the first phase (1962) between minority and majority views at the council. The foundering of the old preconciliar schema on revelation marked the breakthrough of what was to give the Second

Vatican Council its characteristically modern and refreshing stamp, in doctrine as in other things.

1. The church accepts that revelation is a personal communication through the history of salvation. Salvation history enters fully into the concept of revelation and tradition, realities which are no longer narrowly conceived as the intelligible communication of religious truths. Factual and verbal revelation form one entity. Revelation also has a "sacramental" structure.

2. The ancient apostolic church with her scriptures is recognised as a unique event and as foundation of the church; the teaching authority of the church is also subject to God's word, but in its dependence it guides us in our interpretation of the scriptures and of the faith.

3. Not merely the teaching authority but all God's people are the subjects of tradition. Here again the faithful are fully involved in the living mystery which is the church.

4. In carefully chosen terms the critical method of modern exegesis is approved within the bible's fundamental historicity.

5. For the first time in conciliar history the dynamic development of dogma is given recognition.

6. Scripture is the criterium of Christendom's religious life and of the church's preaching.

7. Whereas altar-and-chalice was formerly, as it were, the symbolism of catholicism and, ob-

viously, of the counter-Reformation, the bible is now also taken as a symbol of the Catholic Church alongside the chalice. This dogmatic constitution officially spells an end to catholicism's "counter-reformation" attitude.

Decree on the Apostolate of the Laity

1. New, first of all, is the very fact that there should be a "decree on the laity" in their characteristic, actual situation as members of the one people of God. This means that the layman is taken seriously as a Christian by the "official church", in his task in both the church and the world. Those who were previously "lawless", in the sense that there was not a single official church document for them to refer to, have in this decree received an official status—a declaration to which they can, in religious obedience to the church authorities, appeal, if need be, as of right.

2. This decree is a first official attempt to give a theological definition—at least in the sense of a phenomenological description—of a "Christian layman".

Declaration on Religious Liberty

1. Compared with the official attitude of the church in former times, this declaration reflects an entirely new attitude of mind, based on the

recognition of the unassailable dignity of the human person, down to his personal (perhaps objectively erroneous) outlook on life. The recognition, especially, that everyone may freely and publicly express his philosophy of life, within the changing bounds of the common weal, is something new in the church.

2. Notable also is the church's condemnation of every discrimination in race, colour, conviction, national character, etc.

Decree on the Priestly Ministry and Life

1. This decree transcends the traditional image of the priest, which was defined by his liturgical relation to the eucharist. It draws a pastoral image of him which does not deny his function in religious worship, but incorporates it in a larger entity; the prophetic service of the word and the pastoral leadership and guidance of the church community are thus reappraised.

2. As with the bishops, so also with the priests, all the official functions (not merely the administration of the sacraments) are based on consecration. An official mission is a consecration. The "eastern" aspect, which the West had lost sight of, is thus resumed: priests are ordained, not only to celebrate the eucharist but also simply for *cura pastoralis*, of which the eucharistic celebration forms part, and that as a very central part of it.

3. The priest's spirituality is taken from its monastic framework and based on the official ministry itself.

4. The hierarchy of the church on the one hand throws off its historically developed suspicion of married priests and loyally recognises, for the first time in history, the value of this phenomenon in the eastern churches (for the first time since the Middle Ages, a council document admits that celibacy is not of the essence of the priesthood); on the other it recognises a certain affinity between ministry and celibacy and advocates on this basis the traditional canonical law for the Latin church.

5. In the whole of this document (although it remains "dogmatic" and does not actually enter into the current disquiet concerning the care of souls and the religious ministry) the priest is not surrounded by an aura of mystery but regarded as a real human being.

6. There is a nuanced discussion of the collaboration between priest and layman and (more forcibly still than in the decree on the lay apostolate) of the rights of the laity vis-à-vis their priests.

7. Although the cooperation of (secular and regular) priests with each other and with the bishops lies on a different level from collegiality, the council also stresses the priesthood's essential dependence on the bishops in its entire pastoral mission; coordinated cooperation with the bishop

and, through the guide-lines of the bishop's conference, with the entire national or regional bench naturally follows from this principle. Coordinated cooperation is made structurally feasible by the possibility (in accordance with another decree) of delegates of the higher authorities of the regular clergy attending the decisions on general pastoral planning.

8. Finally, this decree, which is new in many respects, sanctions what we know as "worker-priests", although it uses a different technical term. Thus the council gives its blessing to the priestly life in which manual work is adopted as a form of pastoral presence among men. Compared with the condemnation of the association between priesthood and manual work—almost on the very eve of the council—this is really unbelievably new.

Decree on the Missionary Activity of the Church

1. Although the term "missions" retains the special significance attached to it by tradition (more perhaps from expediency than from any other consideration), this decree nevertheless regards "the missions" as part of the larger "mission" of the church and takes this as its leading thought. "The missions" are not an appendage of the church. There is evidence of a still more pro-

gressive conception where the decree declares that anything it says about "the missions" (countries, that is, which have not yet been historically confronted with Christianity), also applies, to some extent, to former Christian areas which have now become dechristianised; so that, in a theological sense, we could speak of France as a *"pays de mission."*

2. For the first time a council extends the term "missionary" to laymen. And the development task is made part of the missionary activity.

3. New also is the abandonment of the old *commissio* system, under which certain mission areas were regarded, as it were, as the territory of a particular missionary order or congregation. The effect of this was that the local bishop, the real leader of the religious community, could constantly be thwarted in his entire pastoral leadership by another. Coordination remains assured on the ground both of the bishop's advisory council (demanded in another decree) and of the desire (again expressed elsewhere) that, whenever possible, the higher regular clergy should also be given a hearing in the bishops' conferences before any decisions are reached on matters of pastoral planning.

4. Finally, there is at least brief mention of the problem of the *Oikoumenē* in connection with the missionary activities. There also appears a kind of "new style mission", one namely which is no

longer marked by a jockeying for positions of power.

Decree on the Renewal and Adaptation to Modern Times of the Religious Life

Although this decree has fallen short of expectation, it is possible, nevertheless, to detect a few new points which, indeed, lie at its very centre.

1. The "supreme rule" of a monastic foundation is not its own particular "rule and constitution", but Christ himself; the religious life is based on "following Christ", referred to in the bible; in other words, authentic evangelism. That is where the religious life must find its renewed inspiration. The "adaptation of the religious life" must be, first and foremost, a re-evangelising of all its structures. The consequences of this conciliar maxim are more numerous than a superficial reading of it would seem to indicate. The text gives the church an inspiration whose charismatic consequences, I feel, cannot even be surmised at this moment. But eventually this "supreme rule" will break through, without any clashes, we trust, though some may well occur.

2. The second principle imposes limitations, not on evangelism but on unfettered personal conclusions drawn from it within particular religious orders. For, the second guide-line is the

basic inspiration of the religious order or congregation. The original evangelical aspect of a particular foundation must have a place in determining the renewal.

3. There is a reaction against the development of a form of monastic "insularity" within the universal church, as it were, alongside the great biblical, dogmatic, moral-theological, missionary and social tendencies in the universal church.

4. Apostolic monastic foundations in particular must be up to date and show no naïve ignorance about life in the world.

5. New, finally, are the equal voting rights and the complete equality of all brothers and monks and of all sisters among themselves, except for the differences which flow from the priesthood itself.

Pastoral Constitution on the Church in the World of Today

Extensive reference will be made later to this rich if not fully developed constitution. In the meantime the question as to whether there is anything "officially new" in it is relevant here.

1. First of all, its spirit is new. The problem of man's existence functions here in the light of revelation as a really new method on the part of the church authorities. In dialogue with others

they look for a solution in the realities themselves, and so do not appeal to a ready-made "natural law", as it were. This term does not appear once in the conciliar text, whereas in the past, even in *Pacem in terris*, there was a constant appeal to it in this field. The council proves that it finally accepts the historicity of man's existence, and especially that it allows it to function in its thinking of the moral attitudes and actions demanded of us all in the present social situation by man's personal dignity. This is why, except in direct religious affirmations, the constitution no longer strikes a haughty and authoritative tone, as if everything patently derived directly from the natural law. The tone is less pretentious.

2. New also is the fact that Christian anthropology is no longer built on abstract "human nature" but rather considered vocationally; in the sense that man's existence is a vocation and a mission.

3. For the first time the church declares that it not only has something to give the world but has herself much to receive from it.

4. The Christian-anthropological view of the eschatological future of man and his world has undergone a considerable amount of toning down: only paramount certainties are expressed; in company with the world as the world of man, human corporality will have a part to play in the

transfiguration of the divine life—but how this will come about we cannot tell.

5. The whole of this pastoral constitution can be regarded as bringing to an end the "syllabus" mentality of Pius IX. The idea of "Christian secularism" was finally accepted; so, therefore, was the autonomy of secularism on its own ground; as well as the fact that on every Christian rests the duty as a Christian to exert himself for the regulation of secular life as part of his religious practice, so that there is no breach between his life and his religion. Finally, it advocates an "amicable separation of church and state". In other words, medieval politico-social "augustinianism" was thanked for its past services and thrown out.

6. Despite some patchiness due to minority vetoes, the chapter on marriage and the family breathes an entirely new spirit: not only is love recognised as an essential ingredient of marriage, it also plays a part in it as its all-important creative and ethical principle. The controversy around the gradation of the marriage ends is felt to be *dépassé*; the issue is one totality in which, within the marriage project as a whole, love, expressing itself in sexual experience, becomes creative and brings forth the family. Within this love, the dignity of the human person and the very nature of the sexual experience as an expression of love

and, within the context of love, as directed towards the foundation of a human family, are regarded as the ethical principle which is the criterion of the marriage experience. Accordingly, neither the state nor the church nor the priest can decide on the number of children; this is a matter for the consciences of the marriage partners before God and his law. This means that for the first time in her history the church has sanctioned a marriage morality based not on spirituality but on human personality, in which corporality has been adopted precisely as human corporality.

7. Partly new also is that on the subject of earthly possessions the council refers first to the common purpose of all earthly goods and speaks only later and within this framework of the right of ownership. Both capitalism and communism have thus been bridged and at the same time transcended.

8. Further points worth mentioning are the affirmation of the intellectual freedom of research, the fact that social, political or scientific initiatives are to be given a fair chance; and that from a Christian viewpoint, too, there can be pluralism in the adoption of a political and social stand, so that the different groups cannot accuse each other of being worse Christians.

9. Finally, this pastoral constitution is the church's first attempt to define her own position in the complex problems of the world today, an

attempt to initiate a dialogue between the church and the world.

As I have already said, this has been neither an account nor a kind of précis of the basic thoughts of all these council documents; only those aspects which are new to the "official church" have been brought forward. (To be sure, they often coincide with the basic affirmation of these documents.) Moreover, a list could now be drawn up of less happy formulations and of unfulfilled desires— that is to say, not personally expressed desires, but wishes suggested by the disquiet felt in the church as a whole and by living theology. A council can only steer a course on which there is a great measure of unanimity among the bishops and, in the case of more fundamental questions, almost complete unanimity. If the council had pressed on in the face of considerable differences of opinion, there would have been an ever-present danger in post-conciliar times of the bishops in opposition practically paralysing the council decisions. That it was in fact possible to give and take here and there can only be to the good of the active effects and after effects of the council texts in post-conciliar times. And this is precisely what warrants the expectation that the positive and new aspects which have been reviewed here will be put into effect after the council and become a common possession.

My aim in compiling this anthology of what

would, perhaps even without this council, have been alive in many Christians and in theological thinking but without official support and often under constant suspicion, was to encourage those who may be disappointed in the council. Moreover, a scientific and detailed analysis would show us even further, almost unnoticed new aspects: in the approach to ancient religious themes, in the relinquishment of scholastic jargon, in conceptual changes, in the maintenance of ancient concepts in a different contextual perspective, in the omission also of some concepts and traditional terms from truly ecumenical sensitivity, in a certain tendency not to be a Western-Latin council (although this has remained no more than a tendency), in the pastoral concern with which doctrinal texts have been formulated, etc. And if we were to compare the council documents with some of the theological textbooks given to our young seminarians up to twenty years ago (and in use even now in some parts), our tally of points gained would grow considerably larger. That the gains enumerated were made at all despite the uncertain (and originally undreamt of) preconciliar expectations may be a stimulus to us all to seriously read and reflect on the council texts and to discuss them in various clubs and societies.

3

REFLECTIONS ON
THE FINAL RESULTS
OF THE COUNCIL

Anyone browsing through the progressive litera-
ture of the four years which elapsed between the
announcement of the council by Pope John XXIII
around Christmas 1958 and its solemn opening
in October 1962, with an eye for the longings,
wishes and petitions put forward, will be amazed
at the conservatism of even the radical periodicals
of the time. The council, indeed, has gone so
much further that its final result has left those
desiderata far behind. This immediately makes it
clear that the quickened flow in catholic life since
1962, which led to a certain disillusionment in
some quarters with the council achievements, is
due to the conciliar event itself. The appetite has
grown in the eating. From a religious-sociological
viewpoint it further appears that a dynamic movement which finally manages to penetrate deep
down into the ranks of the church leaders, immediately releases every floodgate, whereas its
chances of viability are retarded if it has to lead

a hole-and-corner existence. The conclusion is obvious: excessive tensions between God's people and its leaders can only be avoided by an active and permanent osmosis of the various layers, by periodical councils, with a supplementary permeating structure in the interim periods like the one we now have in principle in the "synod of bishops".

If, in the words of Pope Paul VI at the opening of the fourth session, the doctrinal and pastoral activity of a council is an act of love towards God and man, we may well ask what concrete form this love has received in this council. In drawing up this balance sheet we should distinguish between the result expressed in tabled, approved and promulgated documents; the result of a four-year-long "state of council", i.e. the unfathomable importance of the bishops' contact with each other, with the theologians and with the world press; and, finally, the result of this council viewed in its concrete structure and in the way it actually came through all kinds of tensions. In some respects the latter two facets are perhaps more important than the printed result because they play a greater role in public opinion, which not only reflects the event but also gives this council its image in world opinion. The dynamic energy of the Second Vatican Council, the spirit that moved the world's bishops, clearly transcends the recorded result and guarantees that the post-conciliar period will not be narrowed down to the letter of the council documents.

The sixteen council documents—constitutions, decrees and declarations—can be studied from diverse viewpoints. They can be examined with an eye for the leading thought which consciously or unconsciously guided the entire council theme. This can produce varying results and a certain subjective interpretation cannot be ruled out. Nevertheless, the concrete contents of all the documents may be so considered as to make one aware of a single basic thought which is illuminated from different angles in the various documents. This is not to say that the council itself has consciously and thematically seen, grasped and developed this basic thought. As in the life of humans, so in the life of the church also there are initially more or less unconscious basic intuitions which guide the entire seeking and thinking; it is only in the result that this basic intuition can be thematised or made consciously reflexive. If one tries to do this it also becomes clear that, because the basic idea guided the thinking only implicitly, the end result is not in every detail a balanced and consistent whole. To point this out is my aim in this final discussion.

A council is a religious event. Accordingly the religious quest lies at the centre of every council. It would be wrong to judge this council merely from a new or a conservative theology, from the point of view of the renewal of or adherence to old pastoral methods, etc. Under changing aspects, a council is invariably a reflection on religious matters. The church is indeed essentially a religious manifestation; whatever its historical situation, a council will invariably and exclusively enter a plea for religious matters: "Seek ye first the Kingdom of God." Of that every council is a sign and a witness. The characteristic of Vatican II is that its basic theme concerns the question of religious existence in a world that is changing, abandoning sacral for human forms. This question is developed from all angles: from the world religions, from the Roman Catholic Church, from the *Oikoumenē*, and from all mankind; and in this light I want to outline the council's achievement.

1. Every man's right to organise his life in accordance with his own deepest convictions, subject to the demands of the community's religious welfare, stands foremost. No one, therefore, should be compelled to adhere to any particular religion. But this affirmation of religious freedom does imply that man is also in conscience bound to seek the truth, even in the religious sphere. But religiousness can have no meaning if it does not rest on the free surrender of the heart and on moral conviction.[1]

[1] *Declaration on Religious Liberty*, especially no. 2.

To our modern way of thinking, religious freedom is self-evident. But we should not forget that Christian Europe has for many centuries known bloody persecutions as part of the political struggle for religious truth. The concept of religious freedom is due not to catholic or protestant theologians, but to the jurists and to temporal positive law and, finally, to the modern concept of the democratic state. After some initial difficulties, the traditional catholic conception developed into the so-called concept of toleration which, carefully analysed, is really indistinguishable from article 124 of the Soviet Republic's 1936 constitution; while allowing the faithful freedom of religious practice, this restricts propaganda to the anti-religious citizens.[1] The old catholic concept of toleration allowed only catholics to spread their convictions; the others were only endured to avoid discord. Both cases are based on the conviction: "I have the truth, which alone has rights—and that includes me". The present declaration on religious liberty does not proclaim indifference, but rather respect for the dignity of the human person down to his personal convictions. Seen from a worldly viewpoint, this declaration is undoubtedly the council document which will draw democracy's loudest acclaim; and it removes the cause of the world's suspicion of the church.

[1] F. N. Oleschtschuk, "Atheism," *Grosse Sowjet-Enzyklopädie*, Berlin 1955, 26.

2. The council regards the religious dimension as a constituent of man. Mankind's religiousness is the answer to man's profound thinking on the reason for his existence. Thus the source of all religions lies in a prereflexive, intimately religious awareness, whilst the concrete religions themselves are the varied reflexive or thematised expressions of religious awareness; they are its historical expressions in accordance with the varied genius of nations.[1] Although God is said to have begun manifesting himself as the God of salvation from the very beginnings of mankind,[2] and his redemptive plan extends to all men,[3] the council avoids drawing the non-Christian religions themselves into "the divine plan of salvation", as if they were redemptive institutions desired by God (as the text originally read before its amendment).[4] Some theologians, especially a few French ones, feared that otherwise the non-Christian religions would be placed on the same level of salvation history as Israel or the church of Christ.

But the declaration does state that God's plan

[1] *Declaration on the Relation of the Church to the non-Christian Religions*, no. 1.

[2] *Dogmatic Constitution on Divine Revelation*, chap. 1, no. 3; also *Pastoral Constitution on the Church in the World of Today*, pt. 1, chap. 1, no. 19.

[3] *Non-Christian Religions*, nos. 1 and 2.

[4] *Expensio modorum Schematis "Nostra Aetate"*, Resp. 29, 17. The unamended text read: "de variis salutis depositionibus", which therefore included the non-Christian religions.

of universal salvation, which is not something quite separate from the living reality of concrete humanity, began to unfold as soon as the human race made its appearance on the earth. This indicates that man's search for an answer to the fundamental questions concerning his existence, thematised in the major and other world religions, does not in any case fall outside God's redemptive plan. Anyway, apart from deviations and wrong interpretations, the council sees something unassailable in all religions: all spiritual, moral and social-cultural values in these religions are recognised by the church and she even wants to promote them.[1] Anyone passing from these religions to catholicism need not, therefore, renounce the religious inheritance of his own people. This conciliar affirmation does, however, imply that conversion to Christianity is not a betrayal of the religious and cultural-historical genius of one's own people only in the cases of an Asiatic or an African who does not assimilate Christianity in its western form. Moreover, the *Decree on the Eastern Catholic Churches* and the *Decree on Ecumenism* have emphasised that Christianity's western forms and expressions of thought are not exclusive; the same religious conceptions and dogmas can be expressed differently elsewhere, both as to doctrine and as to the way of life and the whole liturgical experience. This

[1] *Non-Christian religions*, no. 2.

view has enormous consequences for the missionary task of the church, as expressly recognised in the *Decree on the Missionary Activity of the Church*.[1]

For the first time in its history the church has officially relinquished her religious monopoly. This has led to a new attitude to the non-Christian religions and to "searching" mankind in general.

On the other hand, no misunderstanding must be allowed to spring up in connection with this declaration. Its aim is not to give a theology of the non-Christian religions or to take a close look at the problem of the non-Christians' chances of salvation. As the official justification (*expensio modorum*) of the acceptance or refusal of the final amendments expressly states:

> The aim of the declaration is not to give an exhaustive explanation of the flaws in those religions, but rather to show the links between men and their religions as a basis for dialogue and cooperation. This is why the declaration pays especial attention to whatever binds men to each other ... particular consideration is given to what men have in common and therefore leads to neighbourly contact.[2]

Historians of religion would therefore be wrong in their appraisal of this declaration if they were to

[1] Chap. II, art. 3, nos. 15, 16 and 18; chap. III, no. 19; chap. IV, no. 26. See also *Church in World*, pt. 1, chap. IV, no. 44.

[2] *Expensio Schematis "Nostra Aetate"*, no. 1, 13.

accuse it of concealing the shortcomings and imperfections of the non-Christian religions. As the official justification so beautifully puts it:

> The point is not to give the complete truth about the Jews and their religion, but rather to give the complete truth about the bonds between the Jews and the church. This principle is (consistently) applied in the entire declaration on the non-Christian religions.[1]

Nor does all this mean that the declaration does not imply dogmatics. The official justification states: "This declaration means only to give a theological and pastoral basis for a dialogue",[2] and in another passage: "The declaration aims to give not a complete explanation of the other religions but to lay down moral and practical criteria, based on revelation, for a dialogue and collaboration with others".[3] This basic purpose will have to be taken into account if one is not to draw a wrong picture of the declaration or to think it possible, for instance, to build a "theology of Israel" on this council document. It is rich in theological implications, but the possibility of dialogue with non-Christians is its real focus.

3. Compared with the major and lesser non-Christian religions, Christianity is called the "full-

---

[1] *Expensio*, no. 4, 22.
[2] *Expensio*, no. 4, 32.
[3] *Expensio*, no. 4, 21.

ness of the religious life".[1] But Christianity was specially prepared by God's revelation in the Old Testament. Against the background of God's universal redemptive manifestation, commenced when the human race first appeared on the earth,[2] at a certain *kairos* (or moment of grace) in world history, Abraham was called by God to become the founder of a people instructed by Moses and the prophets in pure monotheism and thereafter growing up in messianic expectation.[3] Thus the beginnings of Christ's church lie in the revelation of the Old Testament,[4] and thus Israel was given a place of its own in Christian revelation.

But the revelation was only fulfilled in the person and in the life of Jesus, who through his death and by virtue of his resurrection sent the spirit.[5] Thus Christianity is the final definitive, unrepeatable and no longer surpassable covenant[6]: Christ is the "head of the new and universal people of God's children".[7] He alone is the "mediator and the way to salvation, and in the church, who is his body, he becomes present among us".[8]

[1] *Non-Christian Religions*, no. 2.
[2] *Constitution on Divine Revelation*, chap. 1, no. 3.
[3] *Divine Revelation*, chap. I, no. 3.
[4] *Non-Christian Religions*, no. 4; *Constitution on the Church*, chap. II, nos. 9 and 16.
[5] *Divine Revelation*, chap. 1, no. 4.
[6] *Divine Revelation*.
[7] *Constitution on the Church*, chap. II, no. 13.
[8] *Constitution on the Church*.

The religious experience, thematised in several religions, initially receives its authentic, explicit significance in the Old Testament revelation and finally in Christ, who has established the church among all nations to perpetuate his redemptive work. This then is the council's central affirmation: religiousness receives its basic form, in accordance with God's will, in the "church of Christ"[1]: Christianity in ecclesial form is objectively the mature appearance of all true religiousness. Thus the council has laid down the basic principles for a pastoral approach to present-day humanity, which, though at heart probably still religious or even Christian, is nonetheless abandoning the churches.

While frankly recognising the religious values of all humanity, even as "a preparation for the gospel,"[2] the council clearly affirms, on the ground of the church's faith in Christ, the redeemer, the absolute uniqueness of the Christian religion.[3] The church is the universal sacrament of salvation[4]; "in Christ it is, as it were, the sacrament, i.e. the sign and the instrument of the intimate

[1] *Constitution on the Church*, chap. I.

[2] *Constitution on the Church*, chap. II, no. 16; *Decree on the Missionary Activity of the Church*, chap. I, no. 3.

[3] *Constitution on the Church*, chap. I, nos. 5 and 8; chap. II, nos. 9, 13, 14 and 17; *Divine Revelation*, chap. I, no. 4; *Missionary Activity*, chap. I, no. 7.

[4] *Missionary Activity*, chap. I, no. 1.

union with God and of the unity of the entire human race". The unity in peace, justice and charity, this great powerless longing of present-day humanity, already transcendentally signified in the church itself, even finds its significant realisation in it. It is important, moreover, that the council, speaking of Christ's church, has relinquished the purely hierarchical point of view and is thinking primarily of God's people on its way under the guidance of the hierarchy. Here, too, the stresses have been heavily transposed: the hierarchy itself has relinquished its ecclesial monopoly within the church and attributed this ecclesial character in the first instance to God's people for which it fulfils a ministering guardianship.

The historical confrontation, made possible in our times especially by the world's process of unification,[1] between the other religions and the church of Christ, thus poses more clearly than ever before the problem of this dialogue and of every religion's self-examination. Mindful of its own unique character, however, the church on earth can only regard itself, even in relation to the religiously differently orientated people, as essentially missionary.[2] The missionary activity is, therefore, "an absolute necessity".[3] "The mission-

[1] *Non-Christian Religions*, no. 2.
[2] *Constitution on the Church*, chap. II, no. 17; *Missionary Activity*, chap. I, no. 2; *Non-Christian Religions*, no. 2.
[3] *Missionary Activity*, chap. I, no. 17.

ary activity is none other and no less than the manifestation or epiphany and the fulfilling consummation of God's redemptive will in the world and in history, in which God visibly fulfils the history of salvation through the missionary activity."[1] In the history of the world God manifests, and in his self-manifestation realises and completes, the history of salvation through the mission of the church.

Vatican II's conclusions on religion are, therefore, subtly drawn; while recognising the core of authentic religiousness in all religions, the council maintains the absolute uniqueness of Christ's church, in accordance with the biblical description of this church mystery as "people of God, body of the Lord and temple of the Holy Spirit".[2] This unique biblical church mystery is to be found in the Roman Catholic Church, though veiled and ever open to further clarification[3]:

> Therefore, though not yet embracing all people and often appearing as a tiny flock, this messianic people is nonetheless for all mankind the mightiest germ of unity, hope and salvation. Christ has founded it as a community of life,

[1] *Missionary Activity*, chap. I, no. 9.

[2] *Missionary Activity*, chap. I, no. 5; esp. *Decree on the Priestly Ministry and Life*, Prooemium no. 1.

[3] *Constitution on the Church*, chap. I, no. 8 and chap. II, no. 15.

charity and truth, using it also as the instrument for the salvation of all, and sending it out as the light of the world and the salt of the earth.[1]

The church is, therefore, both a saving community and a saving institution. From this viewpoint, the church as the sacrament of the world's salvation is in principle neither eastern nor western: the church has an eastern or a western aspect according to the people which is shaping her,[2] and through her missionary work, especially in the so-called third world, among the peoples of Japanese, Chinese and African culture, she may take on further aspects still in the future.[3]

4. But as soon as it holds itself up to the world as the sacrament of the world's salvation, Christianity comes up against the concrete historical fact of the division among Christians. The religious problem, therefore, raises the concrete demand for the *Oikoumenē*.[4] Without abandoning her religious conviction that Christ's church as the apostolic fulness is essential for salvation, the Roman Catholic Church in this council has officially given up her

[1] *Constitution on the Church*, chap. II, no. 9.
[2] *Decree on the Catholic Eastern Churches*, nos. 1–16; see *Decree of Ecumenism*, chap. III, nos. 14–17.
[3] *Missionary Activity*, chap. II, art. 3, no. 15; chap. II, art. 4, nos. 19–20.
[4] *Decree on Ecumenism*, Prooemium no. 1; *Missionary Activity*, chap. I, no. 8; *Priestly Ministry and Life*, chap. II, no. 9.

monopoly of the Christian religion or of Christianity. The relinquishment of the exclusive patent not only of religion as such, but also of the Christian religion and, to some extent, even of the only ecclesial form of Christianity (for even non-catholic Christian communities are called "churches" or "ecclesial communities" by this council),[1] inevitably urges the raising of an evangelically purer form of religion peculiar to the church, so that Christ's church can make her legitimate dogmatic claims really true in the eyes of all. This raises the problem of the religious *aggiornamento* of the entire church, both in depth and in breadth.

5. In the *Dogmatic Constitution on Divine Revelation*, the whole church, both the faithful and the hierarchy, places itself more consciously than ever primarily under the critical authority of the primitive apostolic church and her scriptures,[2] without, however, relinquishing the historical development of the church which drew its life from the bible and the saving reality. From this renewed drawing on the bible, the council expects the inner renewal of the entire church.

But nothing more affects the religious experience of Christians than a liturgy which can be

[1] *Decree on Ecumenism*, chap. III, nos. 14 and 19.
[2] "Omnis ergo praedicatio ecclesiastica sicut ipsa religio christiana Sacra Scriptura nutriatur *et regatur* oportet" (*Divine Revelation*, chap. VI, no. 21).

inwardly felt and experienced by the faithful.[1] The start made by the council on the liturgical renewal will cause the spirit of the Second Vatican Council to fill the faithful, especially through the liturgy. The active participation of all the faithful in the liturgy will tangibly show that not only priests and religious, but all are called to the "fullness of the Christian life and the perfection of love".[2]

This attempt to re-evangelise the historical appearance of the entire church can be seen at work in all the ranks of the church, in the priests,[3] in the religious[4] and in the laity.[5] Because, moreover, the principle of the pope's central primacy on the one hand and of the bishops' collegiality on the other (and with it the bishops' conferences) have called a new reality into being, i.e. a pluriform unity in the church, not only has the relationship between "local church" and "universal church" been revised,[6] but it has also become possible for Christianity to become more deeply embedded in a particular national culture. In this way the church can overcome her estrangement from the world.

6. It also raises the whole problem of the re-

[1] See the *Constitution on the Sacred Liturgy.*
[2] *Constitution on the Church*, chap. V, no. 40.
[3] *Priestly Ministry and Life.*
[4] *Decree on the Religious Life.*
[5] *Decree on the Apostolate of the Laity.*
[6] *Decree on the Pastoral Office of Bishops in the Church.*

lations between ecclesially structured Christianity and the world in which we live—a world characterised by its secular activities. This link had already been laid by the *Decree on the Apostolate of the Laity,* which emphasises the sanctity of the laity not only in the church but also in the world's everyday life.[1]

A real appreciation of this religious dimension of life as a gift from God raises the problem of mankind's earthly future and of its absolute future, i.e. of the relation between the organisation of the earthly life and the kingdom of God, announced by the church and confirmed by her among the nations[2]—the field covered by the *Pastoral Constitutions on the Church in the World of Today* (until its promulgation known as Schema 13).

Of that kingdom the church on earth is the germ and the beginning.[3] "In her slow process of development, the church longs for that kingdom in its final fulfilment and strives hopefully and with all her powers towards the final union with her King in glory."[4] This eschatological dynamism of the church,[5] in other words, this striving for the

[1] *Apostolate of the Laity,* chap. I, nos. 2 and 4; chap. II, no. 7; *Constitution on the Church,* chap. IV, nos. 31 and 36.
[2] *Constitution on the Church,* chap. I, no. 5.
[3] *Church in World,* chap. I, no. 5.
[4] *Church in World.*
[5] See also the *Constitution on the Church,* chap. VII, no. 48.

final fulfilment, naturally raises a problem now that present-day humanity has itself discovered its historical, dynamic dimension—has taken its earthly destiny into its own hands and looks ardently to a better future on earth for all men without distinction. Here the problem of "church and world" rises up lifesize. Lost somewhere in Schema 13 are the meaningful words: "The church is the sign and the safeguard of the transcendence of the human person."[1] This can be regarded as the pastoral constitution's basic outlook: man with his transcendental, absolute destiny, though living in an earthly history with its own plans for the future.

Many confusing things have been said about the realities of church and world and various tendencies became noticeable even in the council hall. All kinds of misunderstandings rose to the top and divergent views could be found in the schema itself. Some had in mind a dialogue between the church and the world—as "non-church"—which could only mean "non-believers"—and this at once made humanist and Marxist atheists partners in the dialogue. Others regarded the "world" as the whole secular dimension of life, as all men are called to shape the religious dimension of this same human life within the church of Christ. Again these two views converged in the main intention of this pastoral constitution: the church, i.e. God's people led by its pastors united in coun-

[1] *Church in World*, pt. 2, chap. IV, no. 76.

cil, tries to express in a few fundamental themes her thoughts about the phenomenon of man as a being who, through his own embodiment, realises himself in company with his fellow men in this world, and yet at the same time is personally addressed in the community of his fellow believers by the living God, the bearer of history, who is therefore in his Son made man the alpha and omega of man's stirring history. This formulation summarises not only the material content of the constitution but also its deeper meaning. In the words of its council the church expresses to all who are ready to listen its view of man from the historically conditioned *kairos* of mankind's twentieth-century situation. In this sense the pastoral constitution is a *kerygma* applied to the twentieth-century situation: the evangelically inspired answer to man's empirical question on his present-day problems, expectations and aspirations. The fundamental answer to this double problem of world and church was given in the *Dogmatic Constitution on the Church*, to which reference is also made in the Pastoral Constitution.[1] Its text has already been quoted: "In Christ the church is as the sacrament, that is, the sign and instrument, of the intimate union with God and of the unity of all mankind." The church

[1] Introduction, no. 2. The text from the *Dogmatic Constitution* is quoted in full in the *Pastoral Constitution*, pt. 1, chap. IV, no. 42.

is the effective sign of the mutual unity or fellowship of all mankind through, and in her union with,
God; she is a community among men by virtue of
their communion with the living God. In this universal fellowship the church fulfils a sacramental
role: she is its effective sign. Effective: it is not the
church herself that is in question, but unity among
men; the church is only an "instrument" of God's
redemptive actions in this world and therefore
bound to serve. A sign: this effect is achieved
through the church in a sign, i.e. in this world the
church herself is the pregnant visibility or meaningful presence of an already accomplished (still
accomplishing) community of men in and through
their express communion with God in Christ. In
this sense the church already is the presence of
salvation in our midst, and thus conceived she also
has a value of her own. But, sign and mediating
realisation are one. As a sacrament the church
experiences in advance what still needs to be given
concrete shape in the whole human fellowship.
That means the church achieves a fellowship of
men because she herself is already a community:
God's people and, therefore, a community of
brothers. She is "a sign set among the nations".
The *Pastoral Constitution on the Church in the
World of Today*, as the intrinsic consequences of
the *Dogmatic Constitution on the Church*, has
recognised the existential link between the religious

Christian and the world as a link which is essential to the church yet fades into an unfathomable mystery.

Though still undeveloped, this *Pastoral Constitution* touched the most fundamental problem of our time, popularly presented by John A. T. Robinson, for instance, as well as by many others. Its basic aim is to bridge the gulf between world and religion: "The breach which many bring about between the faith they confess and the lives they lead must be counted among the most serious failings of our time."[1] Reference is here made to the cutting accusation of the prophet Isaiah against "churchy pietists", who "seek (God) daily, and delight to know (his) ways", but do not choose "to loose the bonds of wickedness, to undo the thongs of the yoke, to let the oppressed go free . . . do not share (their) bread with the hungry, and reject their own brother . . ."[2]

Again and again the constitution hammers home that it is precisely through his faith that a Christian bears special responsibility for secular matters and for his fellow man.[3] Its final reflection is reminiscent of the words of Christ that it is not he who prays "Lord, Lord" in orthodox fashion, who will enter into the kingdom of God, but he who also

[1] Pt. 1, chap. III, no. 43.
[2] Is 58:1–12, to which chap. III, no. 43 refers.
[3] See, among others, Pt. 1, chap. III, nos. 34 and 43; in connection with the atheistic dilemma of God or man, also chap. I, no. 21.

gives real effect to his prayer in concrete fellowship. There were some who accused Schema 13 of being too optimistic, while others went so far as to speak of "Teilhardism". But the council document warns against the tendency to identify the development of a world fit for men to live in with the expansion of God's kingdom.[1] The constitution regards the appearance of God's kingdom in worldly features not as coming "from below" but as a gift from above. "Because the mission of the church is a religious one, it is, by that very fact, a highly humanising factor."[2] In this connection the council opposes representations of God and man as competitors.[3] Indeed, "although the same God who redeems us is also our creator, the same Lord of human and of salvation history, not only does this divine policy preserve the rightful autonomy of the creature and especially of man but it also restores and confirms it to its own value".[4] God's kingdom cannot, therefore, be contrasted with the care for man in his concrete historical situation, a care which is, after all, the mainspring of all worldly activities.

The longing for a new world must not hinder the concern to make this earth fit for men to live on but rather stimulate it; for it is on this earth

[1] "Progressus terrenus a Regni Christi augmento sedulo distinguendus set" (Pt. 1, chap. III, no. 39).
[2] Pt. 1, no. 11.
[3] Pt. 1, chap. III, no. 34.
[4] *Church in World*, no. 41.

that lives the community of the new human family which is capable of foreshadowing even now the eschatological kingdom; this kingdom is, therefore, already present on earth in a mysterious form.[1]

Accordingly the consequences of this mysterious presence are clear: "the values of human dignity, of brotherly fellowship and of freedom [note the allusion to *égalité, fraternité, liberté*], all good fruits of our nature and efforts, we shall, after fighting for them here on earth in the spirit of Christ and in accordance with his command, find again later but purified of every blemish, transparent and transfigured—namely, when Christ shall return to his Father the everlasting and universal dominion, 'a dominion of truth and life, of sanctification and grace, a dominion of justice, charity and peace' ".[2]

As a visible community of believers who have expressly gathered around Christ under hierarchical leadership (Pt. 1, chap. IV), the church "to whom has been entrusted the manifestation of the divine mystery, man's deepest meaning in life", must, through this manifestation, "disclose to man the meaning of his own existence".[3] This is the very reason why in Christianity a believer also becomes "more of a man".[4] By its preoccupation with man,

[1] *Church in World*, no. 39.
[2] *Church in World*.
[3] Pt. 1, chap. IV, no. 41; see also no. 40.
[4] *Church in World*, no. 41.

the church stands right in the centre of this world: "Therefore the church proclaims, by virtue of the glad tidings which were entrusted to it, the rights of man and the dynamic energy of the present tide of life, whereby these rights are everywhere promoted, recognised and greatly appreciated" (no. 41). It must, I think, be conceded that these sounds are different from those formerly heard in devotional books on the subject of the world's course. Nonetheless, the council also warns against misconceptions:

> We are, however, exposed to the temptation of considering our personal rights safeguarded only if we cut ourselves adrift from the bonds of divine law. But along that path the dignity of the human person, far from finding salvation, comes to grief.

After discussing the relation of the visible church with the world, the constitution turns its attention to what the religious community in its turn receives from the world. Indeed, for the first time in conciliar history there is a break in the one-way traffic and the church considers not merely the blessings it gives the world, which would apparently know only darkness without and stand outside God's active grace. Now it is also said that the church's religious community develops and grows inwardly richer thanks to man's growing selfawareness and to mankind's new valuable experiences to which it owes much itself—though sometimes rather belatedly.[1] In this connection the council cites, among others, modern social dynamism, the socialising process and man's growing concern for the world's unification; the chapter on culture refers, moreover, to what the development of religious expression owes to the contributions of evolving human awareness.[2] From these worldly contributions the church has learned that she is not bound to a definite culture or political, economic or social system.[3] Therefore, the council now affirms that there can also exist Christian pluralism in secular options. (Pt. 1, ch. IV.) One of the consequences of these views has been formulated by the council:

> Let not the laity imagine that their priests are always so expert that they have a solution to hand for every question, even a most important one, that arises, or that they ought to have one, as if that were their assignment. [Pt. I, ch. IV, no. 42.]

This *Pastoral Constitution on the Church in the World of Today* puts an end to medieval conceptions of the state and of politics.

Reading this whole message against the background of church history, one gets the feeling that it has not been written without causing the church some momentary blushes over her past. The con-

[1] *Church in World*, no. 42.
[2] Pt. 2, chap. II, nos. 58 and 62.
[3] Pt. 1, chap. IV, no. 42.

stitution is loyal enough to acknowledge as much
—in very careful terms—not only as far as the past
is concerned but also the present. "It does not
escape the church how great is the distance between her message and the human weakness of
those to whom the glad tidings have been entrusted."[1] Elsewhere the constitution recalls even
the tragic Galileo case.[2] But the church hopes
to learn from the lessons of centuries of experience.[3] We are listening here to a new spirit, one
rarely heard from official church bodies.

It is impossible to trace here in detail how this
new "secular" spirit, borne by faith in God, the
creator, who is also our undeserved salvation (so
that the entire concrete reality in which we live
comes to us like a grace in the ordinary everyday
things, in the face of our fellow man and in the
great aspirations of humanity today), penetrates
right into the second part of the constitution, which
"in the light of the gospel and of human experience"[4] throws out a few guidelines on five actual
urgent problems of the moment and in the final reflection expressly acknowledges her own imma-
turity. This, however, should be said. If the spirit
of this constitution does not actively and readily
arouse believers—laity, priests and bishops—and
they neither live up to it nor act by it (always under

[1] *Church in World*, no. 43.
[2] Footnote 7 to chap. III, no. 36.
[3] Pt. 1, chap. IV, no. 43.
[4] Pt. 2, no. 46.

the compensating influence of those who *ex-professo* give pregnant shape to the eschatological character of Christianity in the religious life), a new flood of secularism must be feared. For the church will then no longer be able to justify herself in the world today. Instead of sounding the alarm over underground theological tendencies on the part of a so-called "secularised Christianity" (whose spreading waves are indeed noticeable here and there in several countries), it would be better and more effective for us to place Christianity in the middle of our twentieth-century world with its own aspirations and deeply human experiences. There, in the face and in the midst of our fellow men, we could then draw every eye irresistibly to the religious community of the church, because there the so-called outsiders would be able to see at close quarters and in real life what may well be the deepest purpose of their own lives, or at least acquire an eye for the real value of Christianity for mankind. Not without reason the *Pastoral Constitution* has emphasised that the Christians themselves are partly to blame for the general increase of atheism; by their doctrinal representations and their way of living they have obscured and distorted God's image and failed to make the living God sufficiently visible in their lives.[1] The solution to this problem of atheism is, therefore, dependent not only on a purified concept of God but also on the very life of church people themselves.[2]

[1] Pt. 1, chap. I, no. 19.
[2] Pt. 1, chap. I, no. 21.

The paper achievement of Vatican II is certainly considerable, not only in volume but also in tenor and doctrine. While adhering to the dogmatic view of the church as the manifestation of true religiousness desired by God and established in Christ, and, therefore, of the apostolic fullness of Christ's church, the council has given up quite a number of so far more or less consciously held monopolies: authentic religiousness is to be found outside the church, as is explicit Christianity, and even the authentic characteristics of a church; catholics, moreover, no longer identify "the church" with the hierarchy. For the first time in the whole conciliar tradition of the Roman Catholic Church a fourfold monopoly, which the church had assumed with near complacency in a centripetal attitude, often unconsciously, now and then with distinct awareness (as a distorted representation of a true dogma), was expressly abandoned by a new centrifugal attitude; all of this accompanied by a new insight, at least on the part of the official church, which required from many of her adherents a heavy "intellectual sacrifice", namely religious freedom as the affirmation of every man's right to think and live in accordance with his own convictions, subject to the demands of the community's welfare. In view of the church's past, the practical consequences of these five basic affirmations for the future of the church are really incalculable. In my view they will be of more far-reaching significance for the future aspect of the church than Constantine's fourth-century proclamation of Christianity as the state religion was for the history of the West. If we add to this the new openness towards the world, and a more sensitive awareness of the religious and transcendental character of God's kingdom, Vatican II cannot possibly leave the face of the earth unaffected, at least if it does not remain a mere document but becomes a living reality among Christians. Even though we Western Europeans may perhaps regret the mediocrity of documents like those on the communications media, the life in the seminaries, catholic education, the religious life, and, in many respects, even the task of the bishops, these less successful documents cannot take away the importance of the others.

Meanwhile we should not forget that the decree on the seminary life, with its new regulation of studies, means the official ending of the preponderance of scholastic theology in the church; the end, too, of conceptualistic thinking estranged from the bible; and that it makes theological thinking basically biblical once again. An altogether different, more existential approach to the truth—characteristic of all the council documents—henceforth becomes the criterion in the church. And if we mourn over events which we were unable to understand in our hearts and which have sometimes come as a shock to us, in history's memory they will quickly die away. The important things will not be forgotten but receive tangible stature in the church of the future. We could personally meditate on what the council might have been, even on whether the council did indeed touch the real problems of today and what it might have meant to the whole world; we could ask whether many dogmatically sound council pronouncements—to mention one instance: "The church is the sign and the safeguard of the transcendence of man's personal dignity"—do not have a hollow ring on the sound-board of the concrete reality which we behold and sometimes feel to our cost. All this need not be glossed over; the *Constitution on the Church in the World of Today* admits it.[1] The outcome of this council is not a fixed result but a task. Religiousness, Christianity, concern for the church—in the light of God's kingdom and confronted with the world in which we live —those are the basic religious themes of this council and the charge which it lays upon us.

To rise from religiousness via Christian religiousness to religiousness in ecclesial form and to true Christianity, thence to rediscover in ecclesial structures evangelical Christianity and thus to experience anew the authentic core of all religiousness: that seems to me to be the doctrinal-pastoral train of thought of the religious vision deposited in the council documents. Therein lies

[1] Pt. 1, chap. IV, no. 43, especially the last paragraph.

expressed an entire programme for pastoral guidance in the post-conciliar period, a programme also for the catholic "way of life" of the future.

Post-conciliar difficulties

In closing the balance of this council, I cannot refrain from pointing out at least a few of the difficulties which the post-conciliar era will have to face in its efforts to perpetuate and enliven what has been called "the spirit of Vatican II".

1. A careful watch will need to be kept to ensure that no misunderstanding arises around the considerable change of meaning given by Pope Paul VI in his address during the public session of 18 November 1965 to the concept of *aggiornamento* compared with the significance attached to it by Pope John XXIII. To quote Pope Paul: "Henceforth aggiornamento will mean to us: enlightened penetration into the spirit of the Council and the faithful application of the directives so happily and firmly outlined by the council." Before and in the early stages of the council, *aggiornamento* meant throwing open the doors and setting out on a journey of discovery. But in the meantime the council has reached definite decisions, so that from now on the *aggiornamento* is channelled. Herein also lurks the danger of a "post-Vatican catholicism", just as the Council of Trent led to a rigid "post-Tridentine Roman catholicism", at

least if only the second half of the pope's sentence ("faithful application of the council directives") is pounced upon while the first half ("penetration into the spirit of the council") is ignored. Because this means that the criterion of every *aggiornamento* is the apostolic spirit of holy scripture, of which every council—Vatican II included—can only draw an historically situated profile.

2. A second difficulty is connected with the council's key-word: the pastoral character of the council. "Pastoral" was a very ambiguous term in this assembly. During the first session the minority undeniably opposed the pastoral character which the majority wanted to give it. This opposition was due to the rather peculiar meaning of what they understood by "pastoral". Their pleas for a "doctrinal" council soon showed that they regarded an interpretation "doctrinal" and "pastoral" as opposites; which was further confirmed by the interventions from "pastoral" bishops. They held "pastoral" to mean: a practical, apostolically affected attitude which is less concerned with dogmatic or moral truth than with a soothing and encouraging approach to man.

During the second session, the minority became reconciled to the "pastoral" character of the council. But this constituted a threat to its doctrinal value ever since, and even succeeded in making it ambiguous. There was general surprise when, at a given moment, the qualification "dogmatic" disappeared temporarily from the title "dogmatic constitution on the church", after the concept of collegiality had already been approved, at least by an official opinion poll. In other words, an attempt was made to level out the new dogmatic aspects by appealing to the council's pastoral character. Thus the impression was created that the actual doctrine of the church was not to be sought in this council but in earlier ones as well as in the papal encyclicals of this century. This makes it possible to have divergent interpretations of the council documents.

This ambiguity was further increased when representatives of the majority view themselves took to playing with the concept "pastoral". There is no historical sense in trying to deny this. In order to obtain the passage of certain formulations with a modern tendency, they, too, pointed now to the council's pastoral character. And the process was successful. On many points the minority too, convinced that "it was, after all, only a pastoral council", accepted "modern formulations". This gap between "doctrinal" and "pastoral", which was used as a pawn, will continue to have a bearing on the interpretation of the council and is, in my opinion, one of the most important shadows cast on the council debates, to which I have never been able to resign myself. On the other hand, it brought a happy balance in conceptualizing the formulations and definitions of the faith.

3. A third difficulty lies in the "diplomatic choice" of some of the council formulas. These were often selected so as to allow both the majority and the minority to slip in their particular divergent conceptions. One instance will suffice: the council has chosen the expression "unauthorised practices against procreation" in preference to "anti-conceptional techniques". Now, in accordance with the modern viewpoint, it is clear that periodic abstention too can and must be counted among the "anti-conceptional techniques". However, since periodical abstention has already been expressly approved by the hierarchy as a method of birth control in accordance with human dignity, the expression "anti-conceptional techniques" could not be maintained. In consequence, the finally approved formulation "unauthorised practices against procreation" can cover several meanings. Some have approved the formula because they do not want to condemn periodic abstention, others because they want to leave the door open (for instance, for the birth pill) and because, through the formula, they also want to condemn purely egoistical application of periodic abstention. The text is "open", but could be abused.

4. The two preceding difficulties will be weighty ones particularly in the composition of the new

code of canon law. Canon law needs to be guided by faith and theology, not the other way about. The church's past shows that the outward forms of the religious life are really influenced more by current canon law than by living theology. The new composition of the code is therefore of central importance. Owing to the ambiguity of some of the council formulas, even important ones, there is a danger that the translation of council doctrine into canonical laws and forms will start out from the significance attached to it by the minority and not from what the majority meant by it. For this reason, the working commission entrusted with the drawing up of the new code should have a very wide composition and include some theologians.

5. Another difficulty in the post-conciliar period is undoubtedly the possibility of an integralistic reaction, which is, in fact, already springing up in several countries, especially in connection with the so-called Schema 13. Whether this reaction will, in fact, take on violent proportions, depénds, in my view, on two factors: for convenience we can call them "progressives" and "conservatives". On the progressives, in the measure that their legitimate renewed reflection on the faith may neglect the value of obedience as a form of loyal self-surrender. The faith is, after all, a liberating bond, not a liberation from all bonds, however difficult it may be here and now to establish in precise detail

where the bond lies. On the conservatives, in the measure that they, legitimately concerned for the soundness and the authenticity of this bond, identify the treasury of the faith with traditional representations which they cannot give up, with the result that they constantly make their fellow believers suspect. The unavoidable outcome of a clash between these two extremes is integralism. This is why an examination of conscience—their own, not the others'—is called for from both.

6. In connection with the so-called underground theological currents, the soundness of the catholic life will, from a theological point of view, depend in part on whether catholic theologians are in practice given their legitimate freedom of publication and research. If such confidence in theologians does not become a reality, there will be no chance either of their retaining by their dialogue among themselves and by mutual criticism the equilibrium necessary for the reassessment of doctrinal interpretation. For this will lead them, from a sense of brotherly love, to grow intellectually shy of attacking the theories of fellow theologians because of their suspicion that this may lead them into difficulties. The reformed Holy Office or new "Congregation for the Doctrine of the Faith" will, therefore, also need to follow the development of theological thinking in positive ways and allow more room in its own management for free

discussion among theologians. A mere reference to the letter of Vatican II and its consideration as the final norm for the appreciation of theological thinking in the future can only have reactionary results. It can, after all, be regarded as significant that, apart from the constitution on the liturgy (which had been drafted by a working group of wide composition), the other preconciliar schemas in which the contemporary thinking of the Roman centre was largely prevalent, were all written off. Nevertheless, all theological writings of that time were judged from that theological standpoint. Though the council has made up this leeway, the faith naturally remains alive, i.e. theological thinking goes on. If, therefore, the Congregation for the Doctrine of the Faith does not think along the same lines as the faithful, the same distorted relationship will again be revealed in a few years' time.

However, I will not end up in a minor key. It is not in a spirit of what has been termed "le triomphalisme du contretriomphalisme", but in sober assessment of the mentality which came about during the council, that I reach the conclusion: while fully recognising the right of existence of the "Roman viewpoint" within the church, the council has nevertheless clearly shown that this is no longer representative of what is alive in the entire church. The council has laid bare a deep disorder of spiritual communication between the centre and the periphery of the Catholic Church; it has itself already partly removed and in principle healed it on the basis of the permanent bishops' synod and the announced reform of the curia. Thus it is no idle hope that in a not too far distant future both periphery and centre will move on the same wash of the waves, in accordance with the vision of St Ambrose of Milan who saw the whole church as a little boat floating on the waves of world history.[1] *Pusillus grex*, a small flock, but a sign and the forerunner of God's all-embracing mercy.

[1] See Dominican breviary, fourth Sunday after Pentecost: Homilia S. Ambrosii Episcopi (*PL*, 14, 1633).

APPENDIX

Council documents

I. Promulgated at the public session of 4 December, 1963.

    1. Constitution on the Sacred Liturgy ("Sacrosanctum Concilium").

    2. Decree on the Mass Media ("Inter Mirifica").

II. Promulgated at the public session of 21 November, 1964.

    3. Dogmatic Constitution on the Church ("Lumen Gentium")

    4. Decree on Ecumenism ("Unitatis Redintegratio").

    5. Decree on the Eastern Catholic Churches ("Orientalium Ecclesiarum").

III. Promulgated at the public session of 28 October, 1965.

    6. Decree on the Pastoral Office of Bishops in the Church ("Christus Dominus").

    7. Decree on Training for the Priesthood ("Optatam Totius").

8. Decree on the Renewal and Adaptation to Modern Times of the Religious Life ("Perfectae Caritatis").

9. Declaration on Christian Education ("Gravissimum educationis").

10. Declaration on the Relation of the Church to Non-Christian Religions ("Nostra Aetate").

IV. Promulgated at the public session of 18 November, 1965.

11. Dogmatic Constitution on Divine Revelation ("Dei Verbum").

12. Decree on the Apostolate of the Laity ("Apostolicam Actuositatem").

V. Promulgated at the public session of 7 December, 1965.

13. Declaration on Religious Liberty ("Dignitatis Humanae Personae").

14. Decree on the Missionary Activity of the Church ("Ad Gentes").

15. Decree on the Priestly Ministry and Life ("Presbyteratus Ordinis").

16. Pastoral Constitution on the Church in the World of Today ("Gaudium et Spes").

Chronology of the council

1959 *25 January*
Pope John XXIII announces the council.

17 May
Inauguration of preliminaries.

1960 *5 June*
Installation of preparatory commissions and secretariats.

1961 *12–20 June*
First session of the central preparatory commission.

1962 *10 July*
Invitation to other Christian churches to send official observers.

11 October
First public session: Pope John opens the Second Vatican Council in St Peter's.

13–20 October
Composition of commissions (in each case 16 members selected by the Council, 9 appointed by the pope).

Extended to 30 in November 1963 (by 4 elected and 1 appointed member).

20 October–17 December

Debates on schemas on the liturgy, revelation, communication media, the unity of Christians and the church.

8 December

Second public session: closure of first phase; installation of coordinating commission which is to reduce the 71 schemas to 17.

Of these 17 texts only 16 were completed by the council.

See under 20 November, 1964.

1963   *3 June*

Death of Pope John.

21 June

Cardinal Montini becomes pope, adopts the name of Paul VI, announces the continuation of the council.

29 September

Opening of the second phase: third public session.

1–30 October

Debates on the bishops' functions and on ecumenism.

30 October

Tentative voting on the collegiality of bishops and on the revival of the diaconate.

5 November–2 December

Debates on the bishops' functions and on ecumenism.

4 December

Fourth public session; promulgation of:

1. Constitution on the Sacred Liturgy.
2. Decree on Social Mass Media; closure of the second session.

Results of the voting:

1. 2147 for, 4 against
2. 1960 for, 164 against.

1964   *4–6 January*

Voyage of Pope Paul to the Holy Land; meeting with Patriarch Athenagoras, primate of the Orthodox Churches.

17 May

The pope announces the establishment of a secretariat for the non-Christian religions.

14 September

Fifth public session: opening of the third phase.

15 September–20 November

Debates on Mary, the bishops' functions, religious freedom, Jews and non-Christian religions, revelation, lay apostolate, priests, eastern churches, church and world, mission, religious, seminaries, education, marriage.

14 November

Explanatory note on the document on the church.

19 November

Announcement of the 19 amendments to the text on ecumenism.

Voting on religious liberty postponed.

20 November

The schema on the canonical aspect of marriage is referred to the pope after the voting (1592 in favour, 427 against, 5 invalid); important section: mixed marriage.

21 November

Sixth public session; promulgation of:
3. Dogmatic Constitution on the Church.
4. Decree on Ecumenism.
5. Decree on the Eastern Catholic Churches.

Results of the voting:
3. 2151 for, 5 against.
4. 2137 for, 11 against.
5. 2110 for, 14 against.

Pope Paul proclaims Mary as the "Mother of the Church".

Closing of the third phase.

1965   *14 September*

Seventh public session: opening of the fourth phase.

15 September

Establishment of the bishops' synod.

15 September–16 October

Debates and voting on religious freedom, church and world, missions, priests; voting (and detailed amendments) on bishops, religious, seminaries, education, non-Christian religions (including the declaration on the Jews), revelation, lay apostolate.

21 September

Following the pope's intervention the vote was taken on religious freedom.

4–5 October

Pope Paul calls on the United Nations.

11 October

The Pope declares the celibacy law for the priests of the western church an unfit subject for public discussion in the hall.

27 October

First plenary working assembly without debates. From now on there is to be only voting on the remaining documents, with written suggestions for detailed amendments.

28 October

Eighth public session; promulgation of :

6. Decree on the Pastoral Office of Bishops in the Church.
7. Decree on the Renewal and Adaptation to Modern Times of the Religious Life.
8. Decree on Training for the Priesthood.
9. Declaration on Christian Education.
10. Declaration on the Relation of the Church to Non-Christian Religions (including the Jews).

Results of the voting:

6. 2319 for, 2 against, 1 invalid.
7. 2321 for, 4 against.
8. 2318 for, 3 against.
9. 2290 for, 35 against.
10. 2221 for, 88 against, 3 invalid.

10–15 November

The chairmen of bishops' conferences report in the council hall on the conceptions regarding the modernisation of indulgences.

18 November

Ninth public session: promulgation of:

11. Dogmatic Constitution on Divine Revelation.
12. Decree on the Apostolate of the Laity.

Results of the voting:

11. 2344 for, 6 against.
12. 2305 for, 2 against.

Pope Paul announces:

a. the processes of beatification of Pius XII and John XXIII;
b. the reform of the curia, commencing with the Holy Office;
c. the continuation after the council of the three secretariats (for the relations with the other Christians, the non-Christian religions, the unbelievers);
d. a universal period of reflection, from 1 January, 1966 until Whitsun, on the consequences of the council.

6 December

Final working session: final voting on "church and world" and the presentation of a golden ring—a gift from Pope Paul—to all the bishops.

For the first time in history the pope takes part in a service of prayer with the observers from the other churches.

7 December

Tenth public session; promulgation of:

13. Declaration on Religious Liberty.
14. Decree on the Missionary Activity of the Church.
15. Decree on the Priestly Ministry and Life.
16. Pastoral Constitution on the Church in the world of Today.

Results of the voting:

13. 2308 for, 70 against, 8 invalid.
14. 2394 for, 5 against.
15. 2390 for, 4 against.
16. 2309 for, 75 against, 7 invalid.

Reconciliation between the Roman Church and the Orthodox Church by the mutual declaration that the events of 1054 and later are "regretted and consigned to oblivion".

8 December

Final public session: with messages from the council to rulers, thinkers, artists, women, poor and suffering, workers and youth.